Thomas James Mathias

The Shade of Alexander Pope on the Banks of the Thames

Thomas James Mathias

The Shade of Alexander Pope on the Banks of the Thames

ISBN/EAN: 9783337005740

Printed in Europe, USA, Canada, Australia, Japan

Cover: Foto ©Thomas Meinert / pixelio.de

More available books at **www.hansebooks.com**

THE
SHADE
OF
EXANDER POPE
ON THE

BANKS of the THAMES.

A SATIRICAL POEM.

WITH NOTES.

[Price 2s. 6d.]

THE
SHADE
OF
ALEXANDER POPE
ON THE
BANKS OF THE THAMES.

A SATIRICAL POEM.
WITH NOTES.

Occasioned chiefly, but not wholly, by the residence of HENRY GRATTAN, Ex-Representative in Parliament for the City of DUBLIN, at TWICKENHAM, in November, 1798.

Voce fu per me udita,
Onorate l' altissimo Poeta!
L'Ombra sua torna.

Dante Inf. C. 4.

BY THE AUTHOR
OF
THE PURSUITS OF LITERATURE.

SECOND EDITION.

LONDON:
PRINTED FOR T. BECKET, PALL MALL.
1799.

PREFACE.

THIS Poem was chiefly occasioned by the perusal of Dr. Patrick Duigenan's Answer to the Address of Mr. Grattan to his Fellow Citizens of Dublin (a). I considered the Address

and

(a) See " An Answer to the Address of HENRY GRATTAN, Ex-reprefentative of the City of Dublin in Parliament, to his Fellow Citizens of Dublin, by Patrick Duigenan, L.L.D. a Citizen of Dublin, and one of the Reprefentatives of the City of Armagh." 3d edit. with Additions. Dublin, printed for Milliken, Grafton-ftreet, 1798. and for J. Wright, Piccadilly, London.

and the Answer with that attention, earnestness, and zeal which the importance of such a Cause, at this present hour, requires and demands. I considered it in this manner, because whatever affects Ireland, *must* affect the existence and safety of Great Britain, and of all the dependencies, territories, and possessions annexed to the Crown.

I think Dr. Duigenan might have adopted the very words of Cicero against Antony. That Orator requested indulgence and attention when he spoke of himself; but as to the enemy of his country, he exclaimed with confidence; " Cum de illo loquor, faciam ut attenté audi- " atis.(*b*)" A more masterly, just, and irresistible

sistible piece of argument has seldom appeared; and if the eloquence suffers any abatement, it is from the admission of some expressions which might, and should, have been avoided. But a mind intent on great and national matters, urgent in their nature and allowing of no delay, cannot always attend to the minuter elegances and graces of diction.

In Dr. Duigenan's Answer, there is the vigour, the manlinefs, the courage, the impetuosity, the indignation, and the thunder of an orator, feeling for the wrongs of his country, and the horrors of rebellion, againſt a Man, whose political conduct and character have ranked him among the domeſtick enemies of Ireland. Against a man, who appears to have imposed himself upon his credulous country, under the pretence of brilliant talents and rhetorical exertions. Against a man, who boasts that in the hour of distress, *he* EXTORTED from the timid and feeble Minister of the day, and from an improvident British Parliament, such *concessions*, as have been since proved to be inconvenient, and sometimes in direct opposition to the essential welfare of Ireland. Against a man, who received the most extravagant and disproportioned rewards for very equivocal services, and who has now (*c*) fled to England from his own country, from that hue and cry of every loyal subject, which pursued him from the Castle, to the shop and to the cottage.

I have

(*c*) Nov. 1798.

I have nothing to do with Mr. Grattan, but in his publick capacity, as his actions, his writings, and his speeches have demonstrated and declared it to the world. He has signed with his own hand all the doctrines, which have been discussed, exposed, and confuted.

In Mr. Grattan's Address we find, as I think, false facts, even of the day, false history, false reasoning, false premises, and false conclusions. There is inanity of sound, and shallowness of argument. We observe the glosses of the sophist, and all the purple patches in the rhetorician's cloak. It is such a tissue of the most unfounded assertions, rebellious doctrines, and treasonable sentiments, as have discovered, and proved to the loyal subjects of Great Britain and Ireland, WHO AND WHAT

Mr. GRATTAN is. But I refer to the caustick discussions of Dr. Duigenan, whose answer, I hope, will be read in this country; for it does not concern Ireland alone.

When William Wood and his associates had been confounded by the eloquence and energy of Dean Swift, (a man to whom Mr. Grattan bears not the least resemblance in the powers of his mind,) the Copper Captain of that day continued his calumnies in the newspapers. I think that Mr. Grattan has been so examined, so exposed, so probed to the quick in his political capacity by Dr. Duigenan, that his letters, full of sound and fury in the Dublin and London Newspapers, and signifying little, can be considered only as shrieks similar to those of William Wood, in similar agonies. Some of his doctrines, and publick conduct, are briefly exposed in this Poem; as *such* statesmen should be held up to the publick in every point of view, that we may always know who and what they are, and judge them from their own mouth. " Licet omnibus, licet etiam mihi, " dignitatem Patriæ tueri: potestas modo veni- " endi in publicum sit, dicendi periculum non " recuso(*d*)."

I have observed, that this Poem was occasioned chiefly, but *not wholly*, by the appearance and residence of Mr. Grattan in the village of

---

(*d*) Cicero, Philipp. 1.

of Twitnam on the banks of the Thames, the ancient and favourite abode of our great Poet. It is not unnatural to imagine his indignation at such vicinity. No man could have felt greater horror at the scenes of democratick France, the *papal fanaticks*, and rebellious disorganizers of Ireland, and the projected, but baffled, plots of the Jacobins in Great Britain, than Mr. Pope.

To suppose indeed, that the spirits of departed Poets are acquainted with the passing scenes of this lower world, is an indulgence which has always been granted. I think no apology for the supposition can be required or expected. But

But if any person should be so very reasonable, and so very unpoetical as to demand it, I must consign him to the custody of the Governor of Tilbury Fort in the days of Queen Elizabeth, who declared, that no man can see what is not to be seen; or hear, what is not to be heard. (*e*) A sentence indeed of great truth, but which, I fear, would overthrow from their foundation, some of the best poetical fabricks in every language.

It has been declared of SATIRE, (*f*) that " She alone of all her poetical sisters is " unconquerable, never to be silenced, when truly " inspired and animated, (as should seem) from above,

(*e*) Mr. Sheridan's Critick, Act 2.   (*f*) Warburton.

" above, for this very purpose, to oppose (the
" power and influence of) dulness, (conceit,
" democracy, and wickedness) to her very last
" breath." In these days, the various objects which offer, or rather force themselves upon our notice, are very numerous, and many of them are considered in this Poem. But no subject whatsoever is introduced, which has not some reference to the welfare, support, and stability of these kingdoms, and their constitutional government, in this hour of danger and experiment. There is no subject in it which the great moral and national Poet, who is *supposed* to speak, would not have thought worthy either of his casual notice, or of mature consideration, or of jocular allusion and easy pleasantry,

pleasantry, or of his most severe and most powerful Satire. If I have read Mr. Pope's works aright, I think he would, at this hour, have adopted the patriotick words of him, who declared that a Poet was nearly and closely allied to an Orator: " Erigite animos; retinete vestram dig-
" nitatem. Manet illa in Republicâ bonorum
" consensio; dolor accessit bonis viris, virtus
" non est imminuta."(g)

Upon this consideration, if Satire should exalt herself, and if her language should become bold and of ancient potency, it is unjust to attribute it to ill-nature or to malignity. It is the deliberate, keen sensation of a mind feeling for the

(g) Fragment. Orationis in Clodium:
ap. Cicer. Epist. ad Attic. L. 1. E. 16.

the human nature and the human character, for the ruin, the degradation, the confusion, or the disturbance of a well-ordered state, and of that morality and principle which can alone uphold it. It must then be regarded, (as a man whose thoughts were deep, and whose views were clear and comprehensive, once expressed himself,) " Not as malice, but indignation and " resentment against vice and wickedness. It " is one of the common bonds, by which Society " is held together; a fellow-feeling, which each " individual has in behalf of the whole species, " as well as of himself. And it does not appear " that this, generally speaking, is at all *too* " *high* among mankind." When the sustaining principles are in danger, we must look and act beyond ourselves. The connexion of the well-disposed

disposed must be closer than ever; for safety is in coherence alone, and in the order of the state. It is well expressed by Plato, I think in his Timæus, Διακοσμησε, διεταξε, ΞΥΝΕΣΤΗΣΕΝ.

We should feel all selfishness of spirit subdued by the time. We should cast away the petty interests and low considerations of mere literary prudence, and the contemptible submission to half-measures. We should feel them sinking and giving way, when we acknowledge in common with every man who will reflect deeply, what a debt of gratitude we owe to our ancestors who established our Constitution; and how great the duty is of each individual to lend his support to his own country, when publickly attacked or secretly undermined. Resistance must be bold, determined, and

un-

unshrinking, or it is ineffectual; nay, it is worse than no resistance at all. With political knowledge, well or ill understood, is now involved every thing which is valuable and worth preservation. Morality, religion, the laws, literature, our domestick safety, and individual property must perish in the common shipwreck.

In whatever we are at present engaged, the cause is just and righteous. It is a war unsought and unprovoked by our aggressions; a war of self-defence, but extended beyond all powers of our original conception. I hope and trust we shall still be the instruments of a general preservation, and of the deliverance of Europe from the overbearing, desolating, and unrelenting tyranny of France, by a mighty co-operation and an inflexible league.

But

But above all, the internal peace, the quiet, the safety, the authority of the legal powers, the institutions, the manners, and the laws, within the precincts of our own Island, are the most immediate and dearest objects of all our labours, our expences, our arms, and our trophies; worthy of unremitting vigilance, and of united vigour.

Upon the general issue; upon the great united contest; upon the powers of the North, and the strength of the East; on the Isles and the Continents of Europe, and of Asia; on the shores of the Mediterranean; through the Indian and Atlantick waves; on the states of America and the invaded deserts of Africa, the Cause

ONE AND THE SAME is now to be maintained, or lost for ever. There is a voice, (it was the voice of an Imperial Poet the friend of the Minister of his day,) which may be *now* heard with effect by every Nation, but by none with more peculiar emphasis and propriety than by Great Britain and Ireland.

>   Credite nunc omnes, quas dira *Britannia*, Gentes,
>   Quas *Ister*, quas *Rhenus* alit!——
>   Uno tot prælia vincite Bello;
>   Romanum reparate decus, molemque labantis
>   Imperii fulcite humeris: Hic omnia Campus
>   Vindicat; HÆC MUNDO PACEM VICTORIA SANCIT!

November; 1798.

THE
SHADE of ALEXANDER POPE

ON THE

BANKS of the THAMES,

At *TWITNAM.*

A SATIRE;

WITH NOTES.

THE SHADE of ALEXANDER POPE

ON THE

BANKS of the THAMES. (*a*)

" WHAT accents, murmur'd o'er this hallow'd tomb,

Break my repose, deep-sounding through the gloom?

Would mortal strains immortal spirits reach,

Or earthly wisdom truth celestial teach?

Ah!

(*a*) Occasioned chiefly, but not wholly, by the residence of HENRY GRATTAN (Ex-Representative in Parliament for the City of Dublin,) at Twitnam; November, 1798.

Ah! 'tis no holy calm that breathes around:

Some warning voice invites to yonder ground,

Where once with impulse bold, and manly fire,

I rous'd to notes of war my patriot lyre;

While Thames with every gale, or bland or strong,

Sigh'd through my grotto, and diffus'd my song. 10

Whence bursts that voice indignant on my ear?

To Britain ever faithful, ever dear,

E'en *now* my long-lov'd, grateful Country's cause,

Her fam'd pre-eminence, her state, her laws,

Can touch my temper of ethereal mould,

Free as great Dryden, and as Milton, bold.

Sadly the scene I view, how chang'd, how lost!

The statesman's refuge once, and poet's boast;

I hear the raven's hoarse funereal cry,

Since all, whom Ireland spares, to *Twitnam* (a) fly. 20

(a) Mr. Pope generally spelt the word in this manner.

The polish'd Nestor of the classick shore,

Mendip, (*b*) *my* green domain can guard no more;

Lo, Cambridge (*c*) droops, who once with tuneful tongue

The gifts of science, and her wand'rings sung;

With Him, whom Themis and the Muses court,

The learned Warden of the *tatter'd* Fort : (*d*)

For

(*b*) The Right Hon. Welbore Ellis, Baron Mendip, the present possessor of Mr. Pope's villa at Twitnam.

(*c*) Richard Owen Cambridge, Esq. a distinguished veteran in literature and the polite arts. His poem entitled " *The Scribleriad*" is a work of great fancy, just composition, and poetical elegance; but above all, of mature judgment conspicuous throughout. It should be read as well for instruction, as amusement. The preface is entitled to much attention.

(*d*) George Hardinge, Esq. a man of genius and eloquence, M. P. one of the Welsh Judges. He is the present possessor of the villa, called " *Ragman's Castle*" at Twitnam, by the banks of the Thames.

For their best task *my* Sylphs are all unfit,

While more than Gnomes along the meadows flit.

No more my fabled phantoms haunt the plains,

Where Moloch *now*, in right of Umbriel, reigns; 30

His bands from their Hibernian Tophet pass,

And clash the cymbal's visionary brass;

Or round my groves, sublime on murky wing,

Spells of revolt and revolution fling;

And as they glide, unhallow'd vapours shed

On that false Fugitive's inglorious head.

Whence, and what art thou, GRATTAN? has the shock,

And terror low'ring o'er the sable rock,

Hurl'd thee astounded with tumultuous fears,

From Ireland's mutter'd curse, from Ireland's tears? 40

For thee no vistos ope, no friendly glade,

No Muse invites thee to *my* sacred shade;

No airs of peace from heav'n thy presence greet;

Blasts from Avernus, in respondence meet,

Hoarse through the leafless branches howl around,

And birds of night return the obscener sound.

From thee, whate'er thy fame, I spurn all praise;

My lyre ne'er answer'd to Rebellion's lays:

With other lore my purer groves resound,

With other wreaths these temples once were bound;

Nor shall my green sepulchral laurel stand

By Gallick mercy, and a Marian hand.

Hence, and thy baffled Gallick jargon try

On coward slaves, in abject tyranny:

Know, thy *twice-conquer'd* (*d*) Britons still advance;

No chains from Pitt they fear, or humbled France;

From their best source each mingled blessing draw,

Content with freedom, property, and law;

Secure they own their monarch's rightful rod,

His friend, the people; his Creator, GOD. (*e*) 60

Hear then *thy* doctrines, and *thy* patriot love:

" Kings are but satellites; (*ee*) the people, Jove;

" Priestcraft

(*d*) " The English have been conquer'd, *first*, by the Minister, and *afterwards*, by the French." Henry Grattan's Address to his Fellow-Citizens of Dublin. p. 37.

(*e*) " In the people it would *only* be rebellion against *their creature* (the King); in the other (i. e. in the King) it would be rebellion against *his creator*, the people."

Grattan. p. 12.

(*ee*) " Kings are but satellites; and *your freedom* is the luminary which has *called them to the skies.*" Grattan. p. 40. This, I suppose, is a beautiful rhetorical expression alluding to the murder of Louis the Sixteenth, or the modern democratick mode of " *calling kings to the* " *skies.*"

" Priestcraft a falling cause, (*f*) from folly sprung,

" When Saturn reign'd, or when the Pope was young;

" Religion boasts no more a royal rule, (*g*)

" Or great Mathèsis an imperial school.

" Self-legislation (*gg*) to the mob restore; (*h*)

" This is Reform; corruption is no more:

" *Reason*

(*f*) " Priestcraft is a falling cause, and a superannuated " folly." Grattan. p. 22.—If Priest*craft* means the juggling or deceit of Priests, I hope it is falling, and will fall for ever. But I think, no man of sober enquiry and of a cultivated understanding, who admits the truth of Christianity, can ever apply with sense, honesty, or justice, the term Priestcraft, to such an *Establishment* of it, as the Church of England, dependant as it is, on the general law of the land for its support, rights, and constitution. I am here speaking only of the modes of religious worship as they affect civil society, between which there is an important relation, and a close connection —Mr. Grattan's " popular and energetick *Romanists*," could tell him what *Priestcraft* is.

(*g*) " We know of no royal rule for religion or mathematicks." *Grattan.* p. 21. I only notice this, to mark the folly of the rhetorician in it's application

(*gg*) One peculiar feature of Mr. Grattan's inconsistency (now a favourite term) is this: In his Address to the Citizens of Dublin, he recommends and enforces self-legislation,

" *Reason* commands; go, fix *her* limit strong,

" Monarchs are bound, but councils never wrong.

" What legislation, absolute and unqualified, to Ireland; and in his speech on Mr. Fox's motion in the British Houfe of Commons, he asserted and maintained the propriety (and consequently the legality) of Appeals from the Parliament of Ireland to the British Houfe of Commons.

(*h*) " What method remains to limit the monarchy of these kingdoms, Great Britain and Ireland, (it has now no limits) but by Reforming Parliament (i. e. the Houfe of Commons)? What method to *prevent* a Revolution, but a Reformation?" (i. e. of the Houfe of Commons) What is the reformation of Parliament? (i. e. of the H. of C.) but *the restoration* TO THE PEOPLE of *self-legislation?*—Without which there is no liberty, as without reform, no felf-legislation. *So* WE REASONED!!!" Grattan, p. 40. In a preceding part of his Address, Mr. Grattan says, " It is the object of the Reform, that Parliament (i. e. the Houfe of Commons) should continue *in contact* with the people always, and with the Minister never, except the people should be *in contact* with him." Grattan, p. 28. The beautiful

" What *Rights*, by thee proclaim'd, are equal(*i*)shewn?

" Hussey's(*k*)to freedom, BRUNSWICK's to the crown. 72

" Britain

beautiful ambiguity, equivocation, or rather the absolute nonsense, of the word *Contact* suits such an understanding as that of the Ex-Representative of the City of Dublin. "Tantamne rem tam negligenter, tam indiserte, tam impudenter?" Perhaps Mr. Grattan may be of the same opinion with a seditious scribbler, one M'Cormick, concerning the many headed monster, THE IRISH DRAGON, " whose teeth (as M'Cormick tells us) are sown, and " must *ere long* spring up in *hosts of armed Patriots*, " not with frantick rage to point their spears at each " others breasts, but *to fertilize the soil*, and renovate the " proverbial *verdure* of their Country, BY THE BLOOD " of it's cruel oppressors."†—N. B. In the rural œcono- " micks of Democracy, *Blood* is always the manure.

(*i*) " The Catholicks have, in truth and reason, *as good a right to Liberty as* his Majesty has *to the Crown!*" Grattan, p. 21. Such is the sport of a rhetorician with the term *Liberty*.

(*k*) Hussey, the Roman-Catholick, democratick, and seditious, titular Bishop of Waterford. See his *Pastoral* Letter, &c. &c.

Pastorale canit signum! cornuque recurvo
Tartaream intendit vocem.

† See a large pamphlet in 4to. published in 1798, which M'Cormick calls, " The Life of Burke, p. 231.

" Britain no commerce spreads from pole to pole,

" Oppress'd, without an empire to console; *(l)*

" For her no ports expand beneath the line,

" No friendly flags in Arctick splendours join;

" Since Ocean's self republican (*m*) is grown,

" She holds, like Delos, but a floating throne.

" No wisdom in finance, no patriot scheme,

" No modern care in borrowing to redeem, (*n*) 80

" No

(*l*) " The project—to put France at the head of Europe, instead of Great Britain, while her people *crouch* under a weight of debt and taxes, *without an Empire to console*, or a constitution *to cover* them." Grattan, ib. 38.

(*m*) " We saw that these Islands, Great Britain and Ireland, were now two kingdoms in A REPUBLICAN OCEAN," &c. Grattan. p. 39.

(*n*) If Mr. Pitt's principle of *Redemption* in all loans had been originally adopted at the commencement of the Funding System, the National Debt would have been but small even at this period.

" No Constitution *for a cover* (o) left,

" Of rights, of liberty, of laws bereft.

" State-quacks still hold thy prophylacticks good,

" To starve the spirit, (*p*) they remove the food."

Divine Machaon! should thy views extend,

Baker (*q*) must bow, and learned Milman (*r*) bend.

Hence then, and trace the Rhine's polluted flood,

The ruffian plunder, and the price of blood:

Mark the mild guardians of the Gallick land!

Justice, the lion's portion in her hand;   90

         Mercy,

(*o*) See above; Note (*l*).

(*p*) " It appeared to *us*, that the *best* way of starving that spirit, was *to remove the food*." Grattan. p. 16.

(*q*) Sir George Baker, Bart. Physician to the King, of high professional character and learned accomplishments.

(*r*) Francis Milman, M. D. a Physician in London, of great skill and eminence, and extensive practice; a gentleman of classical erudition, polite manners, and of a well-cultivated understanding.

Mercy, in tears o'er fallen sparrows shed,

Beneath her feet the murder'd Monarch's head;

Philanthropy, that fain would fold the globe

With arms fraternal, in a tyrant's robe.

See Directorial Chanceries elate

Stamp their diplomas for each neutral State;

Licentiate Kings in humbled order stand,

Till Rewbell nods, to sweep them from the land.

With horror *now* my purer fancy paints

Ierne's clans, and democratick saints; (*t*)   100

Relicks and rags on Gallick standards fly,

And the *green* rabble of the papal sky. (*tt*)

Oh,

(*t*) "The popular and energetick Romanists, the United Irishmen."   Grattan.

(*tt*) See at large Dr. Duigenan's masterly and irrefragable arguments on the subject of the Roman Catholick religion and principles, in his answer to Mr. Grattan's Address. P. 41 to 45. and p. 123 to 141.

Oh, if Helvetia yet thy soul alarms,

Who mourns her late resolve, and tardy arms;

Pause o'er the fragments of that vengeful storm,

Lo, Rocks, and Ruins, *Rhetors*, and Reform!

Then if one honest pang should rend thy breast,

Look *homeward*—and let Conscience tell the rest.

Hence to the field with Treason's victims strewn;

Reap the dread harvest which *thy* hand has sown:

The robe Prætorian, (*u*) and the learned gown,

Th' insulted Senate, and the loyal town,

(Each smuggled honour from thy temples torn,)

Brand thee alike with epidemick scorn.

Now

(*u*) The freedom of the City of Dublin, &c. &c. &c. has been taken from Mr. Grattan by the vote of the Citizens, Freemen, &c. and his picture removed from the College.

Now loyal flames extend from sire to son;

Cornwallis (*w*) shall compleat, what Clare

begun;

The storm, by awful justice taught to roll,

With Patrick's (*x*) lightning shoot through Grattan's

soul;

One

(*w*) Marquis Cornwallis, Lieutenant Governor, &c. &c. of Ireland. 1798. I cannot better characterize this great and good man, when the tenor of his virtuous and honourable life, and of his publick conduct military and civil, is impartially considered, than in the following lines.

" Non qui præcipiti traheret simul omnia casu;
Sed qui maturo vel læta, vel aspera, rerum
Consilio momenta regens, nec tristibus impar,
Nec pro successu nimius, *spatiumque morandi*,
Vincendique modum mutatis nôsset habenis."

(*x*) See the Answer of Dr. Patrick Duigenan to Mr. Grattan's Addrefs.—I refer to what is faid in the preface to this poem.

One heart, one hand unite each sister realm,
Direct the force, and guide ONE COMMON HELM. 120
Hence, nor presume with hateful steps to rove
By Twitnam's shore, or Windsor's royal grove.

Go rather, and thy wayward measures fill,
" Where *the young Wantons* sport on Anna's hill;" (z)
Blue-bells and red-caps on each bush shall blow,
While Erskine prattles, and while Seine shall flow.

(z) " Or where ye, Muses, sport on Cooper's Hill;
On Cooper's Hill eternal wreaths shall grow,
While lasts the mountain, and while Thames shall flow."
Pope's Windsor Forest.

N. B. St. Anne's Hill is the seat of the Hon. Charles James Fox.

See there the midnight solemn tapers shine,

(So Gilray's (a) patriot pencil rais'd the Shrine;)

While choral Dæmons, from the gulph beneath,

Marseilles' dire notes in hoarser accents breathe, 130

Tartarian anthems! mix'd with sullen moans

Of bleeding martyrs, and rebellious groans.

Mark well the couch, whence Charles from slumber starts

At heads, which Treason join'd, and Justice parts;

Blood-

(a) James Gilray; the political Hogarth of the present day. His pencil has been, and continues to be, of essential service in the publick cause of Great Britain and Ireland. In some of the higher efforts of his genius, such as, " The Sun of the Constitution,—The Homage of Leviathan—The Shrine at St. Anne's Hill," and others which might be named, it is justice to say, that the design, skill, execution, and intention deserve the highest praise. *Multæ Veneris, cum pondere et arte.*

Blood-bolter'd Hamilton *(b)* for vengeance calls,

Vengeance re-echoes from the Castle walls.

Then view the scene, where Charles with senate stir'd,

Stung by contempt, with Gallick phrenzy fir'd,

Shunn'd by the Nobles, by the Commons spurn'd,

While with infuriate thought his bosom burn'd, 140

In treason-taverns bold, address'd the ring,

Bow'd to *his Sovereign*, *(c)* and forgot his King.

But soft; prepare unwelcome truth to hear;

That Botanist *(cc)* may whisper in your ear,

Few

(b) The Rev. and unfortunate Dr. Hamilton, one of the first victims of the Irish Rebellion.

(c) Le Peuple Souverain! as the French Jacobin tyrants term it, and, " The Sovereignty of the People," as the English Jacobins echo it. I am astonished that such nonsensical democratick babble can be endured any longer, even at a tavern from Mr. Barrister Erskine.

(cc) Mr. Fox, the Linnæus of St. Anne's Hill.

Few plants will bear the test of English ground,
It proves the *race* corrupt, the root unsound:
And CRATTAN, mark'd for ever, shall retain
Hibernian forehead, and Hibernian brain.

Time was, when Statesmen, high in fame and place,
With proud distinction *my* retreat would grace; 150
Would court my friendship, soothe my aching head,
By study soften'd, and " with books well-bred;"
Fond to unbend, they sought familiar ease
I never flatter'd, yet could always please.
Then oft with Ministers would GENIUS walk:
Oxford and St. John lov'd with Swift to talk,
Dorset with Prior, and with Queensb'ry, Gay,
And Hallifax with Congreve charm'd the day;

The Muse her Addison to Somers join'd,
The noblest Statesman to the pureſt (*d*) mind. 160

But in these dark, forlorh, distracted days,
Though D'Arcy smil'd, and foster'd Mason's lays,
Few friends are found for poetry and wit,
From North well-natur'd to imperial Pitt.
Yet when his Country's deep-felt intereſt calls,
Himself shall plant the standard on the walls;

Duty

(*d*) Mr. Pope is here supposed to speak of Mr. Addison without remembrance of their jealousies and disagreements; and as Mr. Addiſon deserved of mankind.

" Their tears, their little triumphs o'er,
Their *human paſſions* now no more,
Save Charity, that glows beyond the tomb."

Gray.

Duty (*ee*) shall urge, what talents vainly claim
By native lustre, and untitled name.

But oh, what scenes, what varied wonders press,
What visionary forms my fancy bless!   170
Now fears deject, now blessings round me smile,
The follies, and the glories of the Isle.

Supplies are prompt for Pitt's directing hand;
Pactolus rolls through all the wealthy land;
But still with Tully's speech his wisdom hold,
He never said, *Œconomy is cold*; (*f*)

No

(*ee*) From some late attentions, which have done the Minister honour; and even from the dedication of Mr. Maurice's Second Volume of the History of Hindostan to Mr. Pitt, I am inclined to express the wish of the Poet;

    *Hinc priscæ redeant artes; felicibus inde
    Ingeniis pandatur iter; despectaque Musæ
    Colla levent!*

(*f*) An expression of Mr. Pitt in the H. of C. in November, 1798, imprudent, however qualified. " Magnum Vectigal est Parsimonia," were the words of Cicero. The want of œconomy, (I know what I advance) is the *chief* and prominent defect of Mr. Pitt's administration. With what ease might it be remedied!

No, 'tis the life-blood, feeding all the state,
The source of all that's safe, and all that's great:
Hence Palaces for Bankrupt-Bankers rise, (g)
And Monarchs wonder with enquiring eyes. 180

A voice exclaims, in dread financial search,
" *Commute the Tythes* :" and, lo, a falling Church!
On Sabbath's violated (gg) eve I see
Th' unhallow'd combat, by the murderer's tree:
Reflect, State-Suicides, while Empires nod,
None serve their Country, who forget their GOD.

By Scott unmov'd, behold Ambrosio * stand;
And Lewis braves the justice of the land:

Avonius

(g) Some abuses of this kind should be looked into: what is granted liberally, should be expended wisely.

(gg) Excidat illa dies ævo, ne postera credant
    Sæcula! nos certè taceamus.—

* Ambrosio, or The Monk, a Romance, by M. Lewis, Esq. M. P.—See the Remarks upon it in the Preface to the Fourth Dialogue of the Pursuits of Literature.

Avonius sneaks, his daily progress known,

A rustick hermit peering o'er the town; 190

Carlisle is lost with Gillies in surprize,

As Lysias (*gg*) charms soft Jersey's classick eyes;

Knight (*h*) half-recants; the luscious Darwin sings;

The Baby Rhymer flaps his flimsy wings;

While HE, whose lightest works might soothe the land,

Like the dull ostrich, drops them in the sand.

Through air, fire, earth, how unconfin'd we range!

What veil has Nature? and what works are strange?

All mark each varied mode of heat and light,

From the spare Rumford to the pallid Knight; 200

Though Watson's aid in vain his Chemia calls,

The modest * Hatchett no fatigue appalls;

The

(*gg*) An Athenian Orator, whose works attracted Lady Jersey's attention through the medium of Dr. Gillies's translation. The Oration on Eratosthenes is rather singular.

(*h*) See the Preface to the Second Volume of the Ionian Antiquities published by the Dilettanti Society.

(*) Charles Hatchett, Esq. F. R. S. a gentleman of ingenuity, and of liberal, intense application to the study of Chemistry. The R. S. presented him with their medal for his chemical researches in 1798. Much may be expected from the ability and patient labours of

The Elements contract; the water (*bb*) flies;

Balloons ascend; gas quickens; spirit dies.

Trace all the *rural* whims, that sprout and spread

In branches intricate through Sinclair's head,

Who ships, in ploughs; in oxen, Tritons sees;

The waves, in furrows; and in masts, the trees. (*i*)

Behold from Brobdignag that wondrous Fleet,   209

With Stanhope's (*ii*) keels of thrice three hundred feet!

Be ships, or politicks, great Earl, thy theme,

Oh, first prepare the navigable stream.

The healing Art, to maxims seldom true,

Changes with ease old fancies for the new.

So

(*hh*) Alluding to the experiments of the learned and very ingenious Mr. Cavendish on Water, and it's constituent principles.

(*i*) In allusion to Sir John Sinclair's novel ideas on marine subjects, delivered in the House of Commons some time in Nov. 1798.

(*ii*) The present Earl Stanhope is one of the first experimental Naval projectors in England. He will possibly recollect the proposition he made to a certain Ship-builder.

See Jenner *(iii)* there, the laurel *(k)* on his brow,

Leads up Sabrina's Commutation-Cow! *(l)*

Pasiphaë

(iii) I allude to the present important controversy in the medical world. See the Inquiries by the Doctors Jenner and Pearson, " into the causes and effects of the Variolæ Vaccinæ, or *Cow*-Pox, principally with a view to supersede and extinguish the Small Pox." London, 1798.—The evidence appears as yet to be wholly negative; but it is not my intention to examine all the cases and writings, " *Vaccinus* quæcumque recepit *Apollo*." Dr. Pearson's Treatise is inscribed to Sir George Baker, Bart. which entitles the subject to the consideration of the Faculty. (Nov. 1798.)

(k) This appears from the sublime and poetical words of the ingenious Dr. Pearson; " I would not pluck a sprig of *laurel* from THE WREATH *which decorates the brow* of Dr. JENNER!" Enquiry on the Cow-Pox, p. 3. But still! - Et *Vitulâ* tu dignus et Hic.

(l) Dr. Jenner is a Physician in *Gloucestershire*, and I very naturally suppose that *Sabrina*, the tutelar nymph of the Severn, pointed out to him the fair object of his discovery.

Pasiphäe *(m)* smiles at Syphilitick stains;

But Home *(n)* sheds brazen tears, and Earle *(n)* complains.

Mark

(m) Hic crudelis amor Tauri, *suppostaque* furto
  Pasiphäe, mixtumque genus.   *Æn.* 6.

It is impossible to say, how far the *Commutation System* may be carried in this country. It first began with a little *Tea*, which the celebrated DOCTOR WILLIAM PITT, (a Practitioner of great and extensive reputation, who settled in London about the year 1784, and still continues to give advice to the publick in Downing-Street,) recommended to his Patients, as a cheap medicine in lieu of *light*, *air*, and some other non-naturals. The physicians are now beginning to pay their addresses to the Cow; and the Clergy are afraid that some State-Doctors may offer the same gallant attention to the calves, pigs, and lambs, merely by way of *change*. But if the medical commutation-act is to extend to *other* diseases, I fear that it will be easier for Sir George Baker, Bart. to appease the classical Manes of Fracastorius, than to console some of the medical profession on the extinction of the Nymph Syphilis. (Nov. 1798.)

(n) Everard Home and James Earle, Esqrs. two Surgeons of eminence in London.

Mark now, where bold, with fronts metallick shine
William and *Mary*, (o) on one common coin: 220

Full

(o) WILLIAM GODWIN and MARY WOOLSTONCRAFT GODWIN.—I refer the reader to the Notes in the third and fourth Dialogues of the Pursuits of Literature for the exposition and exposure of Philosopher *William*. At present it is curious to compare the *living* works of Mr. Godwin, with the posthumous writings of the frail fair one; and above all with *the Philosopher's* unblushing account of his own Wife's † amours, life, and conduct. " Ego te ceventem, Sexte, verebor?" Mr. Godwin has fully explained and exemplified what he calls " the most odious of monopolies," Marriage; and has published all his philosophical transactions with *Mary*, previous to his *monopolizing* her. When Mrs. Bellamy's and Mrs. Baddeley's Memoirs were printed, we knew what we were to expect. But when a philosopher, a reformer of states, a guide in *fine* writing, belles lettres, morality, and legislation, like Mr. Godwin, publishes such Memoirs of *his own Wife*, what must we say? " Sic licet tumulo scripsisse, CATONIS MARCIA?"

I have

† See " Memoirs of Mary Woolstoncraft Godwin, by William Godwin.

Full freedom to the genial bed restore,

And

I have been informed, that previous to the important, or as he thinks, unimportant nuptial *contract,* Philosopher Godwin consulted a descendant of Trouillogan in Rabelais, who states in two chapters, (a) " How the Philosopher " Trouillogan *handled the difficulty of marriage;* together " with the answers of that great Ephectick and Pyrrhonian " Philosopher on that subject." A very short specimen of the doubtful doubts, as *handled* by Panurge and that great man, may not be unpleasant or inapplicable.

" Panurge.—Should I marry?

Philosopher Trouillogan.—There is some likelihood.

Panurge.—But if I do not marry?

Philosopher.—*I see in that no inconvenience.*

Panurge.—You do not?

Philosopher.—None truly; *if my eyes deceive me not.*

Panurge.—Yea; but I reckon more than five hundred inconveniences.

Philosopher.—Reckon them, &c. &c.

Panurge.—Well then; *if* I marry, I shall be a Cuckold.

Philosopher.—*One would say so.*

Panurge.—But are you married, Philosopher Trouillogan, or are you not?

Philosopher.—Neither the one, nor the other; and yet both together." &c. &c. &c.

&c.

(a) Rabelais Book 3. Ch. 35. and 36.

And prove whate'er Vanini (*p*) prov'd before.

Fierce

At the conclusion of this Nuptial Dialogue, in which Panurge with all the keenness of his dialecticks pushed the Philosopher home, and probed him to the quick, the great Gargantua, who had heard the whole disputation most patiently from the beginning to the end, non sine stupore, suddenly rose and exclaimed, " Praised be heaven! but above all for bringing the world to *that height of refinedness*, beyond what it was, when I was first acquainted with it; that now the most learned and prudent philosophers are *not ashamed* to be seen entering the porches of the schools of the Pyrrhonian, Aporrhetick, Sceptick, and Ephectick Sects! It will be henceforth found an easier enterprize to take lions by the necks, oxen by the horns, or goats by the beard, than to entrap *such* philosophers in their words!" By which it appears, that the great Gargantua made no allusion, by anticipation, to Philosopher Godwin, who certainly may be *entrapped* with great ease *in his words*, at least in such as he has thought proper to print. But as Panurge said, " Parlons sans disjunctives."

It is however certain, that many parts of this Dialogue must have administered great comfort to Mr. Godwin.

But

Fierce passion's slave, she veer'd with every gust,

Love

But before I can persuade the reader to peruse the Memoirs of *Mary* by her own husband, and all Mary's own posthumous writings revised, and perhaps a little *improved*, by *Mary's* husband, on justice, marriage, rights, wrongs, and so on, to the end of the chapters by "*He and She*", the gentleman and the lady, the *two parties* in the contract; the philosopher and philos*ophess*, the citizen and the citiz*ette*, recourse must be had to abler arguments than any which I can produce. I must request him to study the chapter in which it is shewn, " *How* Pantagruel persuaded Panurge to take " counsel of a fool." Perhaps the Philosopher may here say with Panurge, " Je mettray *mes lunettes* a " cette oreille gauche, pour vous ouïr plus clair."

I still think, that these memoirs and posthumous works of Mary Woolftoncraft Godwin should be earnestly recommended to every father and mother, to every guardian and every mistress of a boarding school throughout the kingdoms of Great Britain,

(48)

Love, Rights, and Wrongs, Philosophy, and Lust:

But is "A convenient Manual of speculative debauchery, with the most select arguments for reducing it into practice;" for the amusement, initiation, and instruction of young ladies from sixteen to twenty-five† years of age, who wish to figure in life, and afterwards in Doctors Commons and the King's Bench; or ultimately in the notorious receptacles of *patrician* prostitution. This is the end of the new school, certain, inevitable, irreversible.

The force of ridicule indeed on this subject can hardly be exhausted upon *the manner* in which these philosophers treat it seriously. The words of Shakspeare press upon the mind;

"I have a speech of fire, that fain would blaze,
But that *their folly* drowns it."

Yet still the consequences are so fatal, and so extensive in their iniquity, that we must also strive to repress them by reasoning, and by every method which learning and reflection can supply or suggest. It is one nefarious system of philosophick *foolery*, which some persons suffer themselves to play with too long, till by

† The Annals of Doctors Commons extend the term.

But some more wise, in metaphysick air,

Weigh

by flowery language, or rather by ridiculous terms, they are at last betrayed into a forgetfulness of original sound principles, and of sober sense. They read, till they persuade themselves, that they can see " the *tear* of " affection (like Mr. Godwin's) *chrystallized* by the " power of *genius*, and converted *into a permanent* " *literary brilliant!!!* (a) But by this nonsense, by this *foolery*, by this substitution of words, aided by the general corruption of morals throughout Europe, the great revolutionary terrors have been brought into action.

Surely parents and guardians should, with the most affectionate earnestness, for the sake of their country, of themselves, of their dearest hopes, and of every institution divine or human, warn and caution young female readers against such writings as Mrs. Woolstoncraft Godwin's; if they perceive an inclination in them to peruse her works. I hate literary prohibitions

---

(a) In *such* language has publick criticism been delivered to the world in one of the Reviews, on Mr. Godwin's Memoirs of his Wife.

Weigh the man's wits (*q*) against the Lady's hair. (*qq*)

Mark in such a case, which are generally ineffectual; but gentle admonition will always have some force on young minds and ingenuous tempers. Their instructors should inform them, that such opinions and doctrines are founded upon the contempt and rejection of that system, which has alone given comfort and dignity to women in the social state, and placed them in honour, confidence, and security.

The Christian code speaks to them of no species of subjection to men, as to masters; but it teaches them to look for support, affection, and comfort from men, as fathers, brothers, and husbands. Is it any wonder, that the Creator should best understand the specifick distinctions, and relations of his creatures? Whatever is consistent with the delicacy of their frame, the care of their minds, the cultivation of their talents, and the superintendence of their family and children, is offered and enjoyed freely and fully by women in this Christian kingdom. These philosophers, of either sex, make marriage the object of their most peculiar ridicule, and then refine it into prostitution.

What

Mark next, how fable, language, fancy flies

To

What can women expect to learn from such writings? To approach them, is to tread, perhaps without design and generally with original rectitude, in the vestibule of the Corinthian temple of seduction and adultery. To no other altars can they be conducted by such a prieſtess as Mrs. Woolstoncraft Godwin. But they should be reminded, that in the gloomy back-ground they may plainly discern the cavern of suicide.

It is unpleasant to criticize, even in the gentleſt manner, the works of the female pen. We have ladies of ingenuity, learning, and of every varied excellence; I would name Mrs. Carter, and Mrs. Hannah More, in the most eminent sense. The genius of the authoress of the Elegy on Captain Cook, the poetry of Mrs Charlotte Smith, and the sombrous fancy and high-wrought imagery of Mrs. Radcliffe, cannot be mentioned without admiration. But when female writers *forget the character* and delicacy of their sex; when they take the trumpet of democracy, and let loose the spirit of gross licentiousness,

To Ghosts, and Beards, and Hoppergollop's (*r*) cries:

Lo,

moral and political, in contempt of those laws, which are their best shield, and of that religion, which has invariably befriended and protected them; the duty which is owing to the defence of our country, and of all female virtue, comfort, and happiness, calls for strong animadverfion. When their softness is laid aside, when they appear as the *Minervas* (*a*) of the modern illuminated syftems, and the Bellonas of France; (*b*) in such cases men must be excused, if they would avoid deftruction even from *their* writings.

Young female readers often find in Mrs. Godwin's treatises a lively fancy, a specious reasoning, a bold spirit, and flights of ideas to which they have been unaccustomed. The possession and the exertion of these ideas they sometimes, in a fatal moment, conceive to be actual liberty, and effectual freedom from restraint,

and

(*a*) Baruel Memoirs of Jacobinism, Vol. 3.

(*b*) Ἁι τ' ἀνδρῶν πόλεμον καταχοιρανεσιν,

Εἰτ' ἀρ' Ἀθηναιη, ατε ΠΤΟΛΙΠΟΡΘΟΣ Ενυω.

Hom. Il. 5.

Lo, from the abyss, unmeaning Spectres drawn, 229

The and the enthralment of prejudice. They drink deep, and are intoxicated with words and fancies, till they are tempted beyond their strength, and become *incapable of their own distress.* Their weedy trophies of liberty, philosophy, and emancipation, fall into the stream together with themselves, their innocence, their comfort, their dignity, and their happiness, to rise no more. (Nov. 1798.)

(p) Vanini, the celebrated atheist, who wished he had been born out of wedlock. " Utinam extra legitimum " torum procreatus fuissem, &c." Such is the blasphemous, idle rant on the subject in his treatise, " De Admirandis Naturæ Secretis."

(q) I shall take my leave of Mr. Godwin (for I have no present intention to examine any more of his works specifically) with some observations on the general tendency of all such authors and their works.

In the present state of civil society, and of political order so wisely established, so vigorously maintained, and so honourably recommended in this still flourishing, opulent, and powerful kingdom; it is difficult to restrain

The Gothick glass, blue flame, and flick'ring lawn!

Choak'd the emotion of the breast, and the indignation of the understanding at such nefarious writings, and desolating principles. The arms, the instruments, and the agents are before us, and are now understood. It was the strong language of Cicero; " Denuncio vitia; " tollite: denuncio vim, arma; removete."* We would recover the health which is gone, and the soundness which is loft. I am of opinion they may both be recovered. But we must all strive, in our several capacities, to direct the vessel of the publick mind, and of the national understanding, in a strait and undeviating course; or, as it is well expressed in one of the Orphick fragments preserved by Clemens, (a) Ιθυνειν Κραδιης νοερον κυτος.

In the sublime, but often fanciful theology, or as I would rather term it, the *Theonomy*, exhibited in the Timæus of Plato, and more fully in the commentary of Proclus, we read of the Εγκοσμιοι Θεοι, or superintending mundane deities. I would not insist upon the imaginary visions of any man, however great; but in the way of

adap-

---

* Cic. Philipp. 1. Sect. 10.
(a) Clement. Alexandrin. L. 5. p. 443. Ed. Lugd. Bat. 1616.

Choak'd with vile weeds, our once proud Avon strays;

When

adaptation, they have often a force and analogy, which is neither unpleasing nor unfruitful. I am sure the present modern philosophical writers, such as Condorcet, and his mongrel disciples in England, Godwin and others, have no pretensions to the reverence of mankind, as mundane deities. Their aim is not to exalt the soul of man, but to depress and degrade it to the beast, or in Sir Thomas More's indignant language, " ad pecuini corpusculi vilitatem." (*b*)

It is remarkable that Sir Thomas More, in his Republick of Utopia, declared that a person who entertained and professed such sentiments, as the modern philosophy holds forth and inculcates, was not worthy to be numbered among rational men, much lefs to be enrolled among the Citizens. His reason was this; that a contempt of all laws and of all institutions was a neceffary consequence of such opinions, when uncontrolled. His words are remarkable: " Illum ne hominum quidem ducunt numero, *tantum abest ut inter Cives ponant*, quorum instituta moresque, *si per metum liceat,*

(*b*) Mori Utopia L. 2.

When Novels die, and rise again in plays:

No *liceat*, omnes floccifacturus sit." † Now we have lived to see, that *fear* has not restrained such *Citizens* as Mr. Godwin and others; and they have accordingly vilified, set at nought, and held out to contempt the laws, the religion, the manners, and the institutions of their country, which defends and protects them, in conformity to the opinion of Sir Thomas More. Such Citizens maintain the doctrines of dissolution, not of compact; the frame and body of Society drops into pieces member after member, when the principle of continuity is withdrawn. " Nigidium vidi; Cratippum cognovi."‡

Men of the greatest minds and of the widest intellectual views, have frequently indulged themselves in forming Utopian Republicks, and have often unadvisedly dwelt too much upon the unavoidable evils of Society. Such pure spirits are naturally offended with every species of evil. Igneus est ollis vigor, et *cælestis* origo. But when such men, as Sir Thomas More, suffer their minds to be

† Mori Utopia, Lib. 2. p. 234. Ed. Glasg. 1750.
‡ Cicero in Timæo, Fragm. de Universitate, Sect. 1.

No Congress props our Drama's falling state,

The

be amused (I fear it is but an amusement at best) with speculative or imaginary political excellence, or rather *perfection*, how different are their *principles*, and the result of their thoughts from those of sciolists and sophists. We all regret the loss of that Republick, which the genius of Cicero had constructed. There are indeed a few noble fragments of the building, preserved by Lactantius, Macrobius, and Augustine; though the plan of the entire edifice by the hand of that consummate practical Statesman, and experienced Philosopher, cannot be traced from the remains. I believe he would have corrected many of the errors of Plato.

But it is not without it's use to compare, (if we have leisure, and as far as we may compare them) the work of the sublimest Heathen Philosopher with that of the Christian Statesman Sir Thomas More. I speak upon

the

The modern ultimatum is, " Translate."

Thence the whole; I am sensible of their errors, particularly in the Athenian: yet when we think of Plato, we must not forget the state of the Heathen world, antecedent to Christianity. But notwithstanding, both these great men proceeded upon the true dignity of the human mind, when undebased by vice; and bottomed their opinions upon the most solid science. Their views were large, comprehensive, connected. They knew the nature and the state of man; and they saw what it would admit, and what it would not bear. When they proposed some amendment, or some institution which did not then exist, it was in the way of suggestion, and not of dogmatical imposition. They never moved through the state with the sword, and the scythe in their hands. What they saw, was with the eye of a well-instructed mind, long prepared by study and exercised in discernment.

These persons in their generations, were indeed among the superintending mundane deities of their country. Not so the modern *Directors* of human affairs; though they aspire to be thought, and to act, as the gods of this nether world. They would sit with the thunderbolt in their

hands

Thence sprout the morals of the German school;

The

hands, and the storms under their feet. Yet even Mythology condemns them, and points to her Salmoneus. But we stand not on the ground of fable: for what is the most extended and the most desolating power of tyrant and of rampant wickedness on the earth, for a few days or a few years, before HIM " who (for his own inscrutable purposes) putteth down and " setteth up, and ALONE RULETH in the kingdoms of " men!"

The consideration of these modern philosophers offers also the strongest argument for the vigorous and unremitting prosecution of *well-directed* study, in all the publick seats of education in these kingdoms. Plato declared, that one of the causes of atheism is, " a certain ignorance " very grievous, which notwithstanding has the appear- " ance of the greatest wisdom." *(d)* This apparent wisdom

---

(d) Αμαθια μαλα χαλεπη δοκεσα ειναι μεγιστη φρονησις. Plato de Leg. . 10.

The Christian sinks, the Jacobin bears rule:

No wisdom must be combated, and overthrown by reason and erudition; the fallacy must be pointed out, and the effect, when perfected, shewn to be DEATH moral, mental, and political.

I am confident that the Universities of Oxford and Cambridge will be still found to be the best and most solid bulwarks (I trust not the only ones) of true science, and of the legitimate cultivation of the understanding, if they adhere to their *original* principles; *but not otherwise*. By this method of reasoning, I should conceive, that the works of Hooker, Pearson, Stillingfleet, and Barrow, have been lately reprinted at the Clarendon press of the university of Oxford, with singular judgment and true discernment of the time. They have been sent forth again into the world, " rejoicing " like giants, to run their course." We are in general either destroyed, or lost, or warped, or led astray, for want of the primal (*dd*) knowledge. I speak not here of the great incontrovertible abstract sciences of the mathematicks,

(*dd*) The words of Plato are worthy of observation. Προς τουτοις, οταν Πολιτειαι κακαι και λογοι κατα πολεις ιδια και δημοσια λεχθωσιν, ετι δε μαθηματα μηδαμη τουτων ιατικα εκ νεων μανθανηται, ταυτη κακοι παντες οι κακοι. Ων αιτιαν οι μεν τες φυτευοντας μαλλον η φιτευομενες, και τας τρεφοντας των τρεφομενων. Plato in Timæo. p. 87. Vol. 3. Ed. Serran.

No virtue shines, but in the peasant's mien,

No maticks, and of natural philosophy founded on a severe and sublime geometry. These cannot be disputed. But I am speaking of the *moral* cultivation of the understanding, that the frame and good order of religion and government may be *still* supported in these realms, by a succession of young men well educated, and judiciously conducted in the paths of erudition. An acute and intelligent observer of history once inscribed a most valuable work *(e)* in these emphatick words: " To the hope of England, its young gentry, is dedicated, the glory of it, its ancient statesmen; a renowned ancestry, to an honourable posterity." I wish to see these words continued, and embodied with strength and energy in Great Britain; her laws will never abhor such a perpetuity.

I have often, when discoursing on education, dwelt with peculiar earnestness on the dignity and wisdom of the Greek writers in almost every department of science, poetry, philosophy, politicks, and morality. I think I have observed, that the modern political theorists, who

are

(*e*) State Worthies; from the Reformation to the Revolution, by David Lloyd; re-published by Charles Whitworth, Esq. in two volumes.

are either not versed in them at all, or but superficially, and who therefore hold them in contempt, have generally wandered the widest and the wildest in these days of confusion, distraction, and convulsion. Aristotle, Plato, and Thucydides, to mention no others, well knew what was the tyrannical nature of a democracy, and all its appendages. None have more strongly or more justly characterized and depicted it; none have held it out to greater reprobation and abhorrence. They teach us alternately by reason, and by example.

The writings of these great men have a perpetual youth. Like the sun, their light is always new, yet always the same; the source of mental life, health, vigour, chearfulness, and fecundity. It guided our forefathers, and it will guide us if we attend to it. The Commentator, or rather the animated rival of Plato, has words which, on such a subject, it is neither unnatural nor improper to produce and to *adapt.*

(63)

Through four dull acts the Drama drags, and drawls,

The

adapt. Οινοχοει αυτοις ἡ Ἥβη. Τον ὁλον κοσμον ὁρωσιν ατρεπτοις και ακλινεσι νοημασι χρωμενοι, πληρουσι τα παντα της δημιεργικης αυτων προνοιας. Συνεστιν αυτοις και ἡ θεοτης, τη μεν νοησει το αχραντον επιλαμπουσα. (f)

I would yet add a few words on these modern philosophers. They sometimes tell us sneering, and in scorn, that the code of Christians is the code of *equality*. They have attempted to shew this more than once. But surely we may ask, what is the equality held forth in the Christian Scriptures? Is it not the equality of the creatures before THE CREATOR? the equality of men before GOD, and not before each other? They every where speak of the distinctions and ranks in society. They ordain tribute to be paid to whom tribute is due; custom to whom custom, honour to whom honour; and they speak of all *lawful* power, as derived from God.

The

(c) Procli Comment. in Timæum Platonis, L. 5. p. 334. Ed. Basil. 1534.

The fifth is stage-trick, and the curtain falls. 240

Lo,

The great Founder of it himself acknowledged the image and superscription of Cæsar. His Apostles declare the gradations of power, delegated by authority; they speak of submission to the ordinances of man, for the Lord's sake; to *the King*, as Supreme; to Governors and Magistrates, as unto them who are *sent by him*. Is this the political equality of the boasted deliverers or oppressors of the world? How long shall we *suffer* the tyrant, the blasphemer, the disorganizing Sophist, to triumph and to *deceive* us?

Finally; when the modern systems are delineated, and the chart of the opinions and doctrines laid out in departments, I would ask, What is the Picture? What are the objects? Are the things recommended and enforced, either true, or honest, or just, or pure, or lovely,

Lo next, where deep within that civick wood,

(No

lovely, or of good report? Is there any thing to be found and felt, but insolent domination; sanguinary, and unrelenting ordinances; and the tyrannical suppression and overthrow of every existing Institution? Throughout the whole of their systems, Is there any virtue, or any praise, or any motive, which the good can approve, and the wise ratify?

I would say, Behold ye despisers, and tremble! I would much rather say to my countrymen; Behold and watch, that ye enter not into the porch and vestibule of their " Plutonian Hall," by the temptation of such Philosophy.

Through the gate,
Wide, open, and *unguarded*, SATAN pass'd,
And all about found, (or made) desolate!

(Nov. 1793.)

(*qq*) Rape of the Lock, C. 5. v. 72.

(r) See an admirable piece of ridicule on the German nonsense of the day, by a man of parts and wit, in a pamphlet entitled, " My Night-gown and Slippers; or, Tales in Verse, written in an Elbow-chair, by George Colman the younger." (Printed 1797.) It is

called

(No balm the trees distill, but lustral blood,)

An called, The Maid of the Moor; or, the Water-Fiend, concerning Lord Hoppergollop's Country House.

But I would refer with still greater pleasure, and the most decided approbation, to " The Rovers, or the Double Arrangement," a Drama in the German style, in the Anti-Jacobin, or Weekly Examiner, No. 30 and 31. A WORK which has been of signal service to the publick, by the union of wit, learning, genius, poetry, and sound politicks.

(rr) The modern productions of the German stage, which silly men and women are daily translating, have one general *tendency* to Jacobinism. Improbable plots, and dull scenes, bombastick and languid prose alternately, are their least defects. They are too often the licensed vehicles of immorality and licentiousness, particularly in respect to marriage; and it should be remarked in the strongest manner, that all good characters are chiefly and studiously drawn from the lower orders; while the vicious and profligate are seldom, if ever, represented but among the higher ranks of society, and among men of property and possessions. This is not done without design.

It is indeed time to consider a little, to what and to whom we give our applause, in an hour of

such

An altar stands: there Tooke his emblems lays,

Shoes, (*s*) razors, constitutions, straps, and stays;

M'Cormick's (*ss*) libel; Wakefield's sanguine gall;

Pitt's rise pourtray'd, (*t*) and the Third Charles's fall;
Historick

such general danger as the present. The Stage surely has the most powerful effect on the publick mind. The Author of *The School for Scandal*, with the purest and most patriotick intentions, long ago endeavoured to make dishonesty, gambling, deep drinking, debauchery, and libertinism, *appear* amiable and attracting in his character of *Charles Surface*; and the German Doctors of the sock and buskin are *now* making no indirect attacks on the very fundamentals of society and established government, subordination, and religious principle; the vaunt-couriers of French anarchy, national plunder, and general misery.

(*s*) The *insignia* of Citizen Hardy, Citizen Kingsbury, Citizen Thelwall, Citizen Tom Paine, &c. &c. and all those philosophers, scribblers, and Lecturers, who serve us

"In a double
    Capacity, to preach and cobble."

(*ss*) Life of Edmund Burke by M'Cormick.

(*t*) Two pair of Portraits, of two Fathers and two Sons, by John Horne Tooke.

Historick scraps of Brunswick or Berlin,

From flimsy Tow'rs, and Belsham's (*w*) Magazine.

There Porson, who the tragick (*x*) light relumes,

And Bentley's heat with Bentley's port assumes; 250

Dramatick

(*w*) Mr. Belsham and Dr. Towers, two Dissenting Compilers of some information and ingenuity, who would be thought Historians.—" They make lame mischief, but they mean it well."

(*x*) RICHARD PORSON, M. A. The most learned and acute Greek scholar of the present age. I allude to his late accurate and most valuable editions of the Hecuba, and Orestes of Euripides, whose integral works may be expected from the Professor. He modestly says, that they are published " in usum studiosæ Juventutis, or, as I suppose, for the use of schools and Tiros.* But his notes and remarks are not adapted to school-boys, to their wants, or their comprehension. He might as well have published them for the use of the Mamalukes in Egypt, or Bonaparte's *Savans*. The Professor should condescend to give some more general illustrations, and a selection of the Greek Scholia.

* Tironum usibus potissimum destinata.
Præfat. ad Hecubam. p. 3.

Dramatick Bardolph in his nuptial noose;

And wiser Perry, (*u*) from his prison loose,

Starts at the Diligence, that tells the tale

How blithe French Printers (*y*) to Guiana sail:

There Scholia, if he would confer a real favour, as it is in his power to do, on the Masters of Schools and the Tutors of Colleges. I hope he will proceed in this important revision, and perhaps effect the final establishment of the Greek text of all the Tragedians. This HE can do, or no man. He will be entitled to the publick gratitude of the *learned* world.—Such a man, so gifted, so instructed, so adorned with various science, I could wish to number among the defenders of the best interests of his country. But at present most unfortunately, in many of our learned men there is, in regard to subjects of political and sacred importance, a something, which, in the phrase of Hamlet, " Doth all the noble substance often *dout*." (*)

Why is it so?

(*u*) Perry, the Editor of the Morning Chronicle, was imprisoned three months in Newgate, for a libel on the House of Lords.

(*y*) The example of the Caravan of *Deportation*, or as it is called from the place of banishment, the *Guiana Diligence* in Paris, should be a warning to the editors and printers of such papers as the Courier, Morning Chronicle, the

* Malone's reading of the passage.

There reeling Morris, and his bestial songs;

Blaspheming Monks; and Godwin's female wrongs;

The Lawyer's strumpet, and *disputed* draft;

And Darwin, fest'ring from the Horatian shaft;

Blossoms of love descend in roseate show'rs,

And last, Democracy exhales in flow'rs. (*yy*)   260

Behold the Star, &c. &c. how they abuse the patience and forbearance of the mild and lenient Government of England.

Under the blessings of French freedom and emancipation, what is the liberty of thinking, speaking, and writing? The authors, the printers, and the booksellers, are crushed at once and equally, and either chained in dungeons, or seized and swept away from their native country, without hope and without judgment, unheard, unpitied, and unknown. Pro lege Voluntas!

But WE have yet a NATION to save; we have millions of loyal men who never bowed the knee to the Baal of Jacobinism; and we have also many who have *drawn back* from the bloody idol, and turned unto righteousness to the preservation of their souls, their bodies, and estates, and the general deliverance of their country.

(*yy*) See Dr. Darwin's Botanick Garden and Loves of the Plants.

Behold La Crusca's Paridel advance,

From Courts, or Stews, from Florence, or from France:

Before him Swift and Addison retire,

He brings new prose, new verse, new lyrick fire;

Proves a designer works without design,

And fathoms Nature with a Gallick line.

But hark! at Pearson's and at Hooker's voice,

The pillars of the sacred dome rejoice;

And hail the day, when Stillingfleet is join'd

To Barrow's vast, immeasurable mind! (z)   270

Geddes

(z) Alluding to the judicious and well-timed republications of Hooker's Works, Pearson on the Creed, Stillingfleet's Origines Sacræ, and a selection of Barrow's Sermons, at the Clarendon Prefs in the University of Oxford, in a convenient form, and for an easy consideration.

Geddes (*a*) may wave his dark Egyptian rod;

Britain still owns th' *inspiring* breath of GOD;

Sees Truth emerge from Oriental (*b*) dreams,

And Gospel treasures roll down Indian streams.

The Dennes, and owlish Stukeleys of the day,

Retire abash'd at Lysons' (*c*) rising ray;

The

(*a*) Dr. Geddes—the Roman Catholick Divine, the new Translator of the Bible.—See some remarks on the Doctor's attempt, in the Preface to the fourth Dialogue of the Pursuits of Literature.

(*b*) See the Asiatick Researches, in particular those by Sir William Jones, and Mr. Maurice's Indian Antiquities, and his History of Hindostan, which have afforded the most curious and important facts, if applied with judgment and soberly investigated.—But we may expect a work on the Sacred Writings, of the greatest importance, and of the deepest erudition and ingenuity from a Gentleman, whom I shall not name. Yet perhaps, " Nunc intelligitur, olim nominabitur."

(*c*) I cannot but observe, that the learned world has much to expect in the improvement, reform, and conduct of the

study

The Macedonian march, the Libyan state,

On Rennell's (*d*) keen decisive labours wait;

And see each grateful Muse on Vincent (*e*) smile,

His kindred talents, and congenial toil.   280

Pitt

study of Antiquity, from the genius, erudition, difcernment, active age, and unceasing diligence of SAMUEL LYSONS, Esq. F. R. and A. S.

(*d*) I allude to the works so long and so eagerly expected by the learned, from that consummate Geographer, and most accurate investigator, Major JAMES RENNELL.

(*e*) The Rev. WILLIAM VINCENT, D. D. Master of Westminster School. A Gentleman whose professional merits, deep erudition, and unwearied application to science, in the intervals of a laborious and honourable calling, demand the most decided teftimony of publick approbation. I believe, I fpeak the general fense of every scholar in the kingdom. Surely an honourable retreat, and some distinguished mark of publick gratitude, should be offered *in time* to such men, as Dr. Vincent, who have devoted their talents and attainments to the

publick

Pitt once again revolves the Stagirite,

And bends o'er Plato by *Serranian* light;

Philosophy uprears her ancient head,

And Grecian truth in Grecian words is read;

Arts, Arms, and Policy maintain their course,

And Science flows from her primæval source.

But now I feel th' avenging thunder roar,

In British terror on the dusky shore;

The publick service, with unremitting diligence. The Masters of our great schools should be made *independent, in every sense, of their scholars*. This would stamp a dignity and firmness on their office and on their character, and the kingdom would derive great advantage from such a regulation.

I believe it is impossible to name such a work as Dr. Vincent's Translation of the Voyage of Nearchus, with all the learned illustrations, produced under the labour and constant pressure of so important an occupation, as the conduct of a great publick school. It has been received at home and abroad with equal attention and honour.

The Bog Serbonian (*f*) yawns for Gallia's doom;

And Pompey points to Bonaparte's tomb!

There, as in mournful pomp o'er Egypt's woes,

Th' embodied Majesty of Nilus rose,

In sounds of awful comfort NELSON spoke,

And the Palm wav'd obeisance to the Oak;

Firm, yet serene, the Christian Victor rode,

And on his flag inscrib'd, THE WILL OF GOD! (*g*)

The

(*f*) "That Serbonian Bog,
Betwixt Damiata and Mount Casius old,
Where Armies whole have sunk." P. L. b. 2.

(*g*) The Victory of Admiral Lord NELSON on the First of August, 1798, over the French Fleet on the shores of the Nile; that signal interposition of the Divine Providence.

" Illi *Justitiam* confirmavere triumphi;
PRÆSENTEM docuere DEUM! nunc Sæcula discant
Indomitum nihil esse pio, tutumve nocenti!"

The guilty Nation shakes; her trophies fall:
The Crescent nods; and Selim yields to Paul:
The Hellespont expands in timely pride;
Fleets not her own adown the current glide;   300
The North-Star beams on Europe's parting night,
And the dawn reddens with effectual light!

I go: my Country's fate no more I mourn;
And pleas'd revisit my august sojourn."

———

Nov. 1798.

THE END.

A TRANSLATION

OF THE

PASSAGES

CITED IN THE

PREFACE AND NOTES

TO THIS

POEM.

MOTTO TO THE POEM.

Voce fu per me udita,
Onorate l' altissimo Poeta!
L'Ombra sua torna.   *Dante Inf. C. 4.*

" I heard a voice saying unto me, Pay honour to the mighty Poet! *His shade is returning.*"

CITATIONS IN THE PREFACE.

P. 2.

Cum de Illo loquor, faciam ut attentè audiatis.
Cicero Philipp. 2.

" When I speak of the man himself, I will take care to ensure your attention."

P. 7.

Licet omnibus, licet etiam mihi, dignitatem Patriæ tueri; potestas modo veniendi in publicum sit, dicendi periculum non recuso.
Cicero Philipp. 1.

" It is the right of every man, it is even mine, to endeavour to support and vindicate the honour and dignity of his country; and while I have the power of appearing before the publick, I decline not the danger of delivering my sentiments openly and boldly."

P. 11.

Erigite animos; retinete vestram dignitatem. Manet illa in Republicâ bonorum consensio; dolor accessit bonis viris, virtus non est imminuta.

Cicero Fragment. Orationis in Clodium, ap.
Epist. ad Attic. L. 1. E. 16.

"Raise up your minds; maintain your own dignity and high estimation. There is still throughout the state an unity of sentiment among the good; well-disposed men have been deeply affected at the scenes which have passed before them, but their virtue and spirits have suffered neither abatement, nor diminution."

P. 13.

Διεκοσμησε, διεταξε, ξυνεστησεν.

Plato in Timæo.

"He disposed, he arranged all things, and then gave them consistence and stability."

P. 16.

Credite nunc omnes, quas dira *Britannia*, Gentes,
Quas *Ister*, quas *Rhenus* alit!—
    Uno tot prælia vincite bello;
Romanum reparate decus, molemque labantis
Imperii fulcite humeris; Hic omnia Campus
Vindicat; hæc pacem mundo Victoria sancit!

"Give attention and credit to my words, all ye People, whether in *Great Britain*, on the *Danube*, or on the *Rhine*.—

By one great engagement supersede the necessity of so many contests; restore the glory of *Rome*, and support the weight of the falling *Empire*. This one field avenges all your wrongs; this one victory ratifies the peace of the world!"

NOTES

CITATIONS
IN THE
NOTES TO THE POEM.

P. 27.

" Tantamne rem tam negligenter, tam indiferte, tam impudenter?"

" Is it not shameful to treat so important a subject with such negligence and carelessness, such inattention to propriety of speech, and with such effrontery?"

P. 27.

Pastorale canit signum! cornuque recurvo
Tartaream intendit vocem.

" He sounds the *pastoral* note, the signal of onset; and sends forth a blast as from Tartarus."

P. 32.

Non qui præcipiti traheret simul omnia casu;
Sed qui maturo vel læta, vel aspera, rerum
Consilio momenta regens, nec tristibus impar,
Nec pro successu nimius, *spatiumque morandi*,
Vincendique modum mutatis nosset habenis.

" He was a man who would not hasten the ruin of all things by precipitate and fatal violence; but who knew well how to temper and adjust the alternate preponderance of good and evil, by maturity of counsel. He was not depressed by adversity, or inflated with insolence by success; but by prudent management according to circumstances, he had the skill to pause with propriety, and set bounds to the profecution of victory."

P. 34.

P. 34.

Multæ Veneris, cum pondere et arte.

Hor. A. P.

" Compositions of great beauty, with the skill of a master, and the dignity of a moralist."

P. 38.

Hinc priscæ redeant artes! felicibus inde
Ingeniis pandatur iter, despectaque Musæ
Colla levent!

" May we behold again the revival of the ancient arts! may the way be opened for the promotion and encouragement of all rising ability and genius, and may the Muses once more emerge from a state of dejection, depression, and neglect!

P. 39.

Excidat illa dies ævo, ne postera credant
Sæcula! nos certé taceamus.

" May that day perish from the records of time, that Posterity may never credit the report! We shall pass it over in silence."

P. 42.

Vaccinus quæcunque recepit Apollo.

" All the writings of which have been received into the *Vaccine* Repository."

P. 42.

Et Vitulâ tu dignus et hic.   *Virg. Ecl.*

" Either of you are worthy of the prize, the female calf."

P. 43.

P. 43.

Hic crudelis amor Tauri, suppostaque furto Pasiphäe.   *Æn.* 6.

"Here are recorded the cruel love of the Minotaur, and the clandestine substitution of Pasiphäe."

P. 44.

Sic liceat tumulo scripsisse, CATONIS MARCIA?   *Lucan. L.* 2.

"Must we *thus* inscribe on the tomb, here rests the Marcia of Cato?"

P. 52.

Ἀιτ' ἀνδρῶν πόλεμον κατακοιρανέουσιν,
Εἴτ' ἄρ Ἀθηναίη, εἴτε πτολίπορθος Ἐνυώ.

Hom. Il. 5.

"Such goddesses as preside over the wars and contentions of men, whether Minerva, or Bellona who lays cities in waste and desolation."

P. 54.

Denuncio vitia; tollite: denuncio vim, arma; removete

Cic. Philip. 1. *Sect.* 10.

"I declare and denounce publickly to you the specifick vices and crimes; take them away: I declare to you the force intended, the arms, and the instruments; remove them."

P. 54.

Ἰθυνειν κραδιης νοερον κυτος.

Fragm. Orph. ap. Clement. Alexandr. L. 5.

"To direct the intellectual vessel of the heart."

P. 55.

Ad pecuini corpusculi vilitatem.

Mori. Utop. L. 2.

" To the vileness of the bestial body."

P. 55.

Illum ne hominum quidem ducunt numero, *tantum abest ut inter cives ponant*, quorum instituta moresque, *si per metum liceat*, omnes floccifacturus sit.

Mori. Utop. L. 2.

" They do not consider him among the number of rational men; so far are they from enrolling him among the citizens, whose institutions and manners he would ridicule and set at nought, if not restrained by fear."

P. 56.

Nigidium vidi; Cratippum cognovi.

Cicero in Timæo. Fragm. de Universitate.

" I have seen the philosopher Nigidius; and I was acquainted with Cratippus."

P. 59.

Ἀμαθια μαλα χαλεπη, δοκουσα ειναι μεγιστη φρονησις.

Plato de Leg. L. 10.

" A certain ignorance very grievous, which notwithstanding has the appearance of the greatest wisdom."

P. 60.

P. 60.

Πρὸς τουτοις, ὅταν Πολιτειαι κακοι και λογοι κατα πολεις ιδια και δημοσια λεχθωσιν, ετι δε μαθηματα μηδαμη τουτων ιατικα εκ νεων μανθανηται, ταυτη κακοι παντες οἱ κακοι. Ὧν αιτιατεον μεν τους φυτευοντας μαλλον η φυτευομενους, και τους τρεφοντας των τρεφομενων.

Plato in Timæo. p. 87. *Vol.* 3, *Ed. Serrani.*

" Added to this; when bad political institutions and pernicious doctrines are the subjects of lecture and discourse from city to city in publick and in private, and when instructions and sciences, by no means calculated to remedy the evil and counteract the fatal influence, are instilled into the rising youth; this is the reason why those who are of bad dispositions, continue to be bad. We must blame the planters, and not the things planted; and reprobate the instructors rather than the instructed."

P. 63.

Οινοχοει αυτοις ἡ Ἥβη. Τον ὁλον αισθητον κοσμον ὁρωσιν ατρεπτοις και ακλινεσι νοημασι χρωμενοι, πληρουσι τα παντα της δημιουργικης αυτων προνοιας. Συνεστιν αυτοις κυριδιη Θεοτης, τω μεν νοκσει το αγηραντον επιλαμπουσα.

Procli Comment. in Timæum Platonis,
L. 5. *p.* 334. *Ed. Basil.* 1534.

" Hebe, the goddess of Youth, presides at their entertainments. They comprehend with the eye of the intellect the whole sensible world; and by thought and intention of mind, which is never warped or turned aside, they fill all things by a species of creative wisdom and foreknowledge. They have always a youthful divinity; and the power of their understanding shines forth with a brightness not subject to diminution."

P. 75.

P. 75.

Illi *Justitiam* confirmavere triumphi;
Præsentem docuere Deum! nunc Sæcula discant
Indomitum nihil esse pio, tutumve nocenti!

Claudian; on the fourth Consulate of Honorius.

"These triumphs and these victories have confirmed and ratified the cause of *Justice:* they have taught and evinced the presence and the interference of God! May hence all ages and all nations learn, and feel, that no power can finally prevail over the virtuous and the pious; and that there is no state of stability or of security for the blasphemous and the wicked!"

THE END.

This day is published,

1. In One Volume Octavo, a new and Complete Edition, being the EIGHTH, revised; to which is prefixed An INTRODUCTORY LETTER TO A FRIEND, on the general Subject of the Work,
(Price 8s 6d in Boards)
THE PURSUITS OF LITERATURE.
A SATIRICAL POEM IN FOUR DIALOGUES, WITH NOTES.

---

2. A TRANSLATION OF THE PASSAGES from Greek, Latin, Italian, and French Writers, cited in the NOTES to the PURSUITS OF LITERATURE, a Poem in Four Dialogues. To which is prefixed,
A PREFATORY EPISTLE,
Intended as a GENERAL VINDICATION OF THAT WORK from various Remarks which have been made upon it.
BY THE TRANSLATOR.
Price 2s 6d in Boards.

---

3. The IMPERIAL EPISTLE from KIEN LONG, EMPEROR OF CHINA, to GEORGE the THIRD, KING OF GREAT BRITAIN, &c. &c. &c. in the year 1794.
Transmitted from the Emperor, and presented to his Britannick Majesty by his Excellency the Right Hon. George Earl Macartney of the Kingdom of Ireland, K.B. Ambassador Extraordinary and Plenipotentiary to the Emperor of China in the Years 1792, 1793, and 1794. Translated into English Verse from the Original Chinese Poetry. By the Author of
THE PURSUITS OF LITERATURE.
With Notes by various Persons of Eminence and Distinction, and by the Translator.
Ignotum Ratalis carmen caleque Latino
Fingimus, et finem egressi legemque priorum.
JUV. SAT. VI.
THE FOURTH EDITION, PRICE 1s 6d.

Printed for T. BECKET, Pall-Mall.

www.ingramcontent.com/pod-product-compliance
Lightning Source LLC
Chambersburg PA
CBHW020302090426
42735CB00009B/1187